MW00903940

THIS BOOK BELONGS TO:

COLOR TEST PAGE

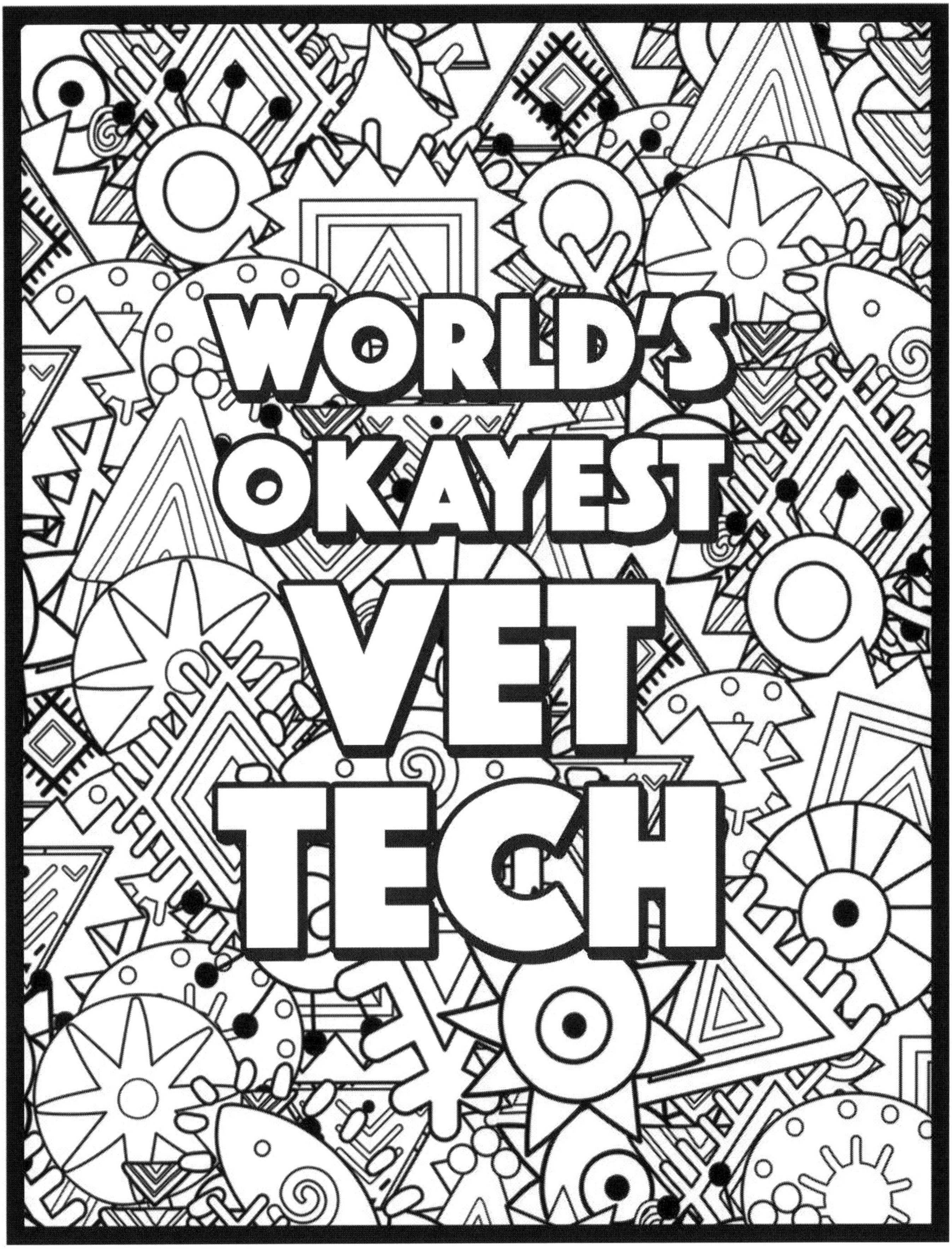
WORLD'S
OKAYEST
VET
TECH

I NEVER DREAMED I'D BE A SUPER COOL VET TECH BUT HERE I'M KILLIN' IT!

I'M NOT
RESPONSIBLE
FOR WHAT
MY FACE DOES
WHEN YOU
TALK

I'M
PAW
SOME

INSTANT
VET
TECH
JUST ADD
COFFEE

MAKE
Today
MAGICAL

SOME PEOPLE
JUST NEED A
HIGH-FIVE
(IN THE FACE)

YOU MUST
BE MISTAKING
ME FOR A
VETERINARY
TECH
WHO GIVES A
SHIT

FRIDAY.
MY 2ND
FAVORITE
F WORD.

SORRY
I'M DONE
HELPING
ASSHOLES
TODAY

KEEP CALM
AND
SQUEEZE A
Toebean

TIRED-ASS
Vet
Tech

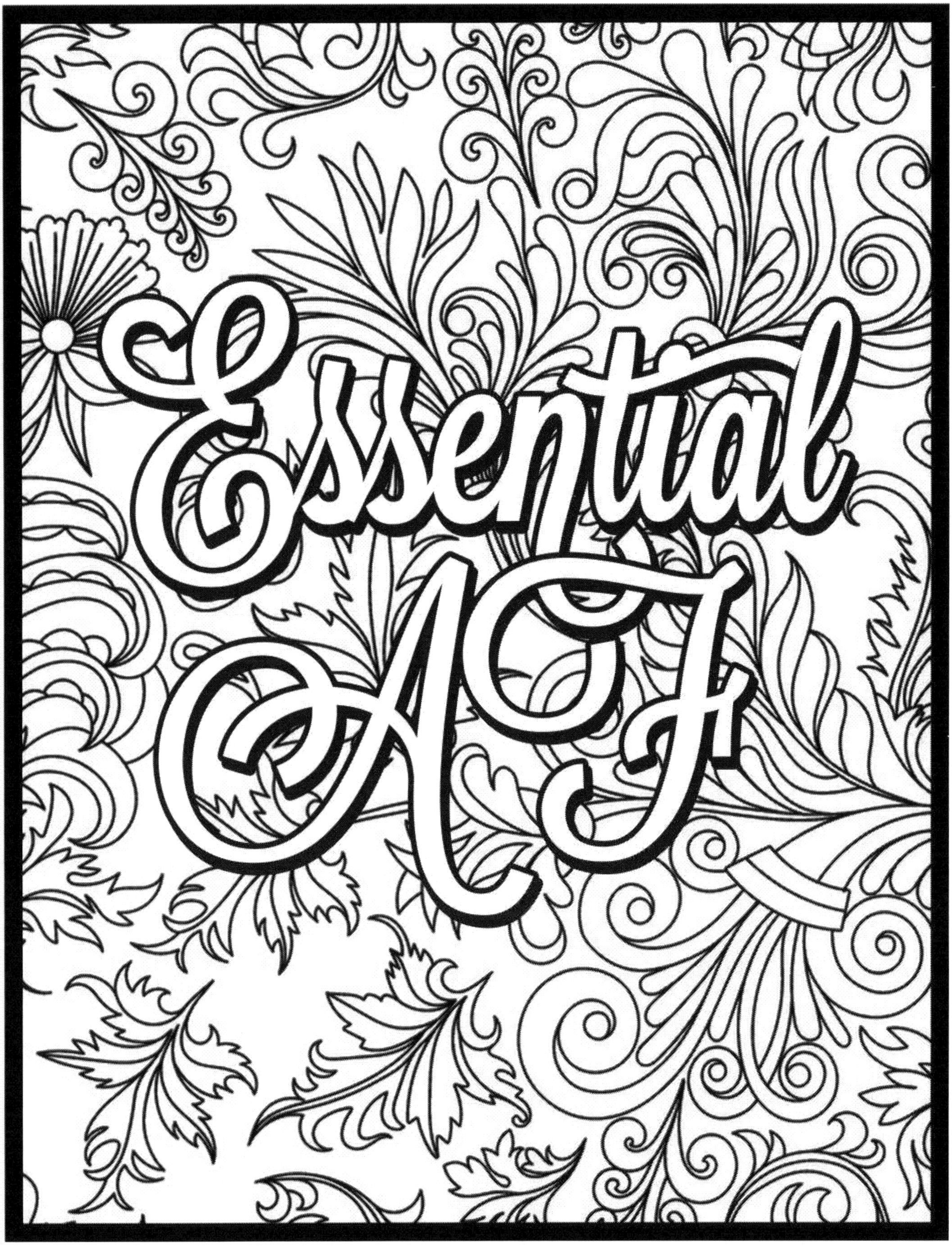
Essential
AF

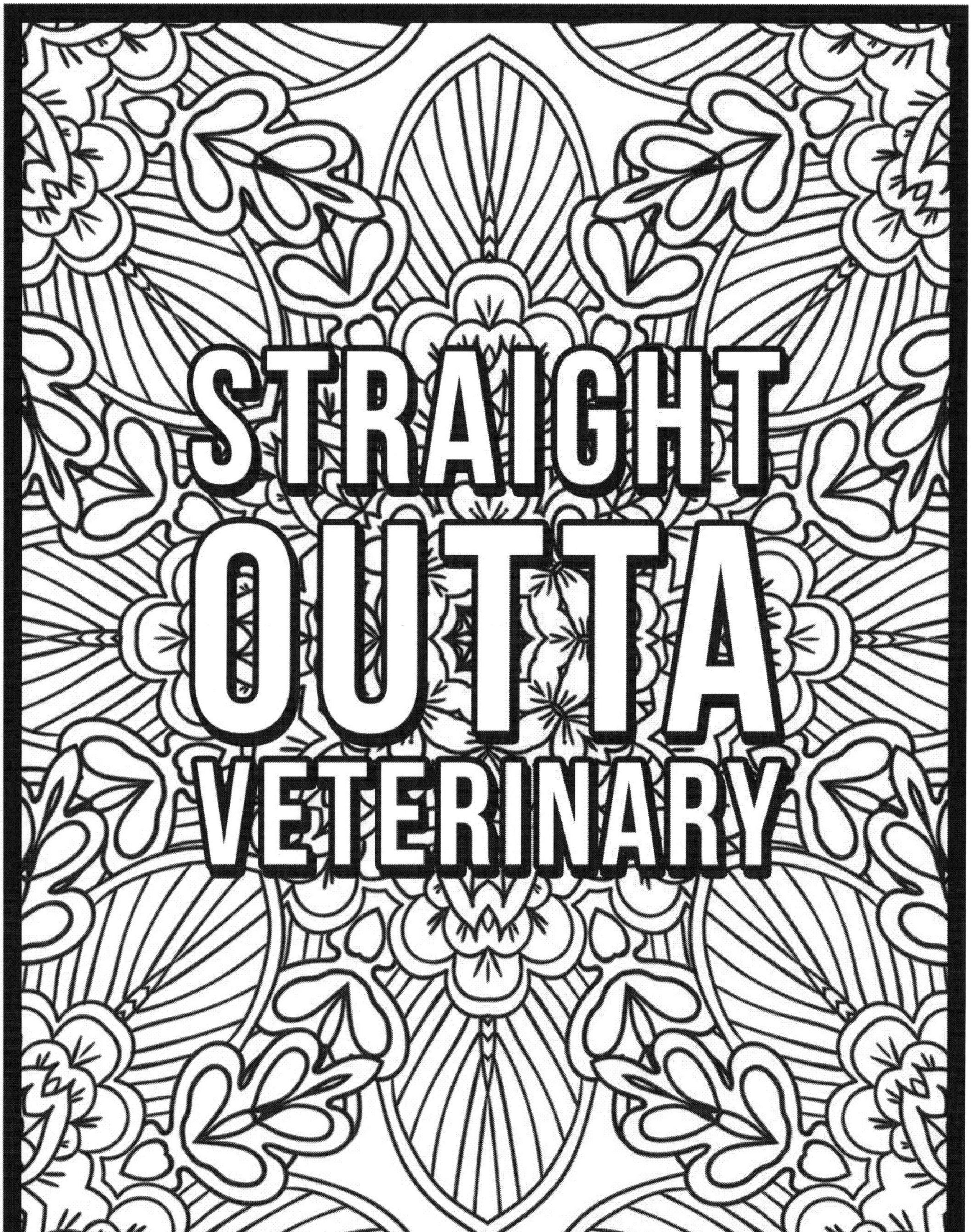
STRAIGHT
OUTTA
VETERINARY

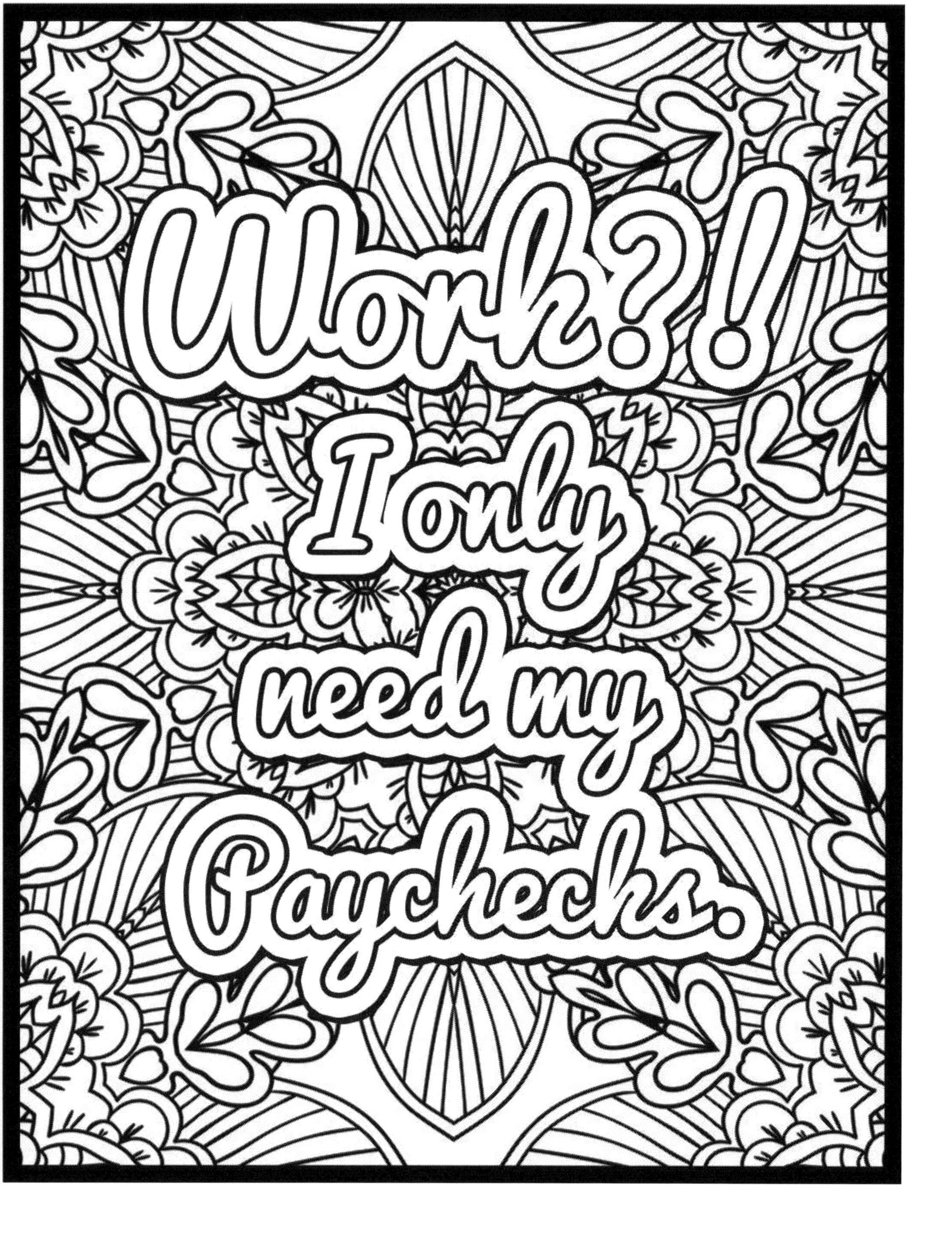
Work?!
I only
need my
Paychecks.

Be Nice
Or I will
Muzzle
YOU

I'VE 101
PROBLEMS
BUT
COLORING
AIN'T ONE

I can't fix
Stupid
But I can
Fix what
Stupid
Does

I'm a
Nice Person
Just Don't
Push my
Bitch
Button!

Fat
Pet
Talk

Made in United States
Orlando, FL
15 December 2024

55732467R00026